WHAT IS A COMMUNITY?

JEANNE NAGLE

Britannica
Educational Publishing

IN ASSOCIATION WITH

ROSEN
EDUCATIONAL SERVICES

Published in 2018 by Britannica Educational Publishing (a trademark of Encyclopædia Britannica, Inc.) in association with The Rosen Publishing Group, Inc.
29 East 21st Street, New York, NY 10010

Distributed exclusively by Rosen Publishing.
To see additional Britannica Educational Publishing titles, go to rosenpublishing.com.

First Edition

Britannica Educational Publishing
J.E. Luebering: Executive Director, Core Editorial
Mary Rose McCudden: Editor, Britannica Student Encyclopedia

Rosen Publishing
Heather Moore Niver: Editor
Nelson Sá: Art Director
Matt Cauli: Designer
Ellina Litmanovich: Book Layout
Cindy Reiman: Photography Manager
Heather Moore Niver: Photo Researcher

Library of Congress Cataloging-in-Publication Data

Names: Nagle, Jeanne, author.
Title: What is a community? / Jeanne Nagle.
Description: New York : Britannica Educational Publishing in Association with Rosen Educational Services, 2018 | Series: Let's find out! Communities | Audience: Grades 1-4. | Includes bibliographical references and index.
Identifiers: LCCN 2016056465| ISBN 9781680487350 (library bound book : alk. paper) | ISBN 9781680487336 (pbk. book : alk. paper) | ISBN 9781680487343 (6 pack : alk. paper)
Subjects: LCSH: Communities--Juvenile literature.
Classification: LCC HM756 .N34 2017 | DDC 307--dc23
LC record available at https://lccn.loc.gov/2016056465

Manufactured in the United States of America

Photo credits: Cover, pp. 1, 4, 8, 29, interior pages (background) Rawpixel/iStock/Thinkstock; p. 5 SerrNovik/iStock/Thinkstock; p. 6. sabthai/iStock/Thinkstock; p. 7 oneinchpunch/iStock/Thinkstock; p. 9 opolja/iStock/Thinkstock; p. 10 sergioboccardo/Shutterstock.com; p. 11 Jupiterimages/Photos.com/Thinkstock; p. 12 Comstock Images/Stockbyte/Thinkstock; p. 13 TOSHIAKI ONO/a.collectionRF/Thinkstock; p. 14 DebraMillet/iStock/Thinkstock; p. 15 TAGSTOCK1/iStock/Thinkstock; p. 16 gemenacom/iStock/Thinkstock; p. 17 projockphoto/iStock/Thinkstock; p. 18 Chris Lawrence/Alamy Stock Photo; p. 19 Ron Chapple Stock/Ron Chapple Studios/Thinkstock; pp. 20, 22, 23, 26 monkeybusinessimages/iStock/Thinkstock; p. 21 Digital Vision/Thinkstock; p. 24 Highwaystarz-Photography/iStock/Thinkstock; p. 25 Jupiterimages/Creatas/Thinkstock; p. 27 Adam Taylor/DigitalVision/Thinkstock; p. 28 Tanya Constantine/Blend Images/Thinkstock.

CONTENTS

What Community Means

Community is a word that means different things to different people. Each community is unique. Yet they all have things in common. A community can be a group of people living in a particular area. A community can also be a group of people with common interests who may or may not live together.

A community can be made up of a large or small group of people. The land area of a community can also be large or small. A

When people come together, they often do so as part of a community.

VOCABULARY

Unique means being the only one of its kind.

community may be roomy or crowded, depending on the size of its land area and how many people live there.

Every community has boundaries. Boundaries can involve the actual space a community has or uses. Rules about membership or behavior within the community might also create boundaries.

People can, and often do, belong to more than one community at a time.

A community can be as small as a family or a group of friends.

GETTING AND GIVING

Members of a community live, work, play, and learn as a group. Community members often band together to reach goals or to get things they need or want. The things they need can include goods and services. Goods are items that people use, and services are things people do for others.

However, being in a community is not just about getting something. Members also have to give back to make sure that a community is successful.

Teamwork is one thing that is necessary to make a community successful.

Each person has a role to play. Some people may be leaders who organize community activities. Others show their support by sharing their time, talent, or treasure (money or goods). They might volunteer their time to clean up their neighborhood or they might teach others a new skill. All members also contribute by being on their best behavior and following community rules.

Projects to beautify or clean up an area require community members' time and effort.

THINK ABOUT IT

Community services include school systems, garbage disposal, and libraries. What other community services do you or your family use regularly?

SUCCESSFUL COMMUNITIES

Some communities are more successful than others. Their members are happy and they work well together. People have studied different communities to find out why some work better than others. They have found that most successful communities have four things in common.

Members of successful communities feel as if they belong and have things in common with others in their community. Community members also should feel as if they have influence in the group. They want to be able to make a

Meeting to discuss issues and make plans helps all members feel involved in their community.

difference, both through and within the group.

Happy communities have members who bring different skills and views to the community.

Finally, members of a community should share history, experiences, and time together. These connections create important bonds. People cannot truly come together, and make good things happen, if they do not like and trust each other.

Community members share many things, including their thoughts and ideas.

VOCABULARY
Influence is the power to change someone or something.

GEOGRAPHIC COMMUNITIES

There are many different kinds of community. One of the most common is a geographic community. This kind of community is formed by many people living close together in the same area.

Geography is a science that deals with Earth's surface. Physical geography describes the land and its features. Features are things like mountains, lakes, and deserts. They affect how each community is built and survives.

The mountains in Alberta, Canada, are part of the province's geographic landscape.

Physical geography greatly affects how communities function. For instance, how might life be different for people living in a desert community versus people living near a rainforest?

Human geography describes how groups of people live within geographic areas. Human geographers might study why communities develop in certain places. Others study a community's culture, including customs, languages, and religions.

Geographic communities are defined by physical boundaries, or limits, as well as how the people within them live. Examples of geographic communities include cities, towns, villages, and neighborhoods.

A family enjoys a walk—and run—through their neighborhood.

CITIES

Cities are made up of many people from different backgrounds that live closely together within set boundaries. However, geography is not the only thing shared by these communities. People who live and work in cities share resources and services, and everyone must also obey the city's laws.

There is often a pattern to how cities are built. In the middle of the city is usually an area called

Some laws, such as the one requiring seatbelts, are designed to keep community members safe.

the downtown. This area has office buildings and big stores. Cities also may have one or more areas of factories and storage buildings outside of the downtown.

Cities also have houses and apartment buildings, where people live. Throughout the city are places where people can relax and have fun. These places include restaurants, museums, parks, and theaters.

THINK ABOUT IT

Public transportation, such as buses or trains, is one type of shared service in a city community. Can you think of others?

Because of the resources available there, downtown areas are frequently busy, day and night.

Towns and Villages

Big cities are called urban areas. Geographic communities called suburbs are located near big cities. They can be towns, villages, or small cities.

Towns are considered local communities, meaning community members live and work closely together within a small, set space. They share local services and facilities. Smaller than cities, towns tend to have more houses and apartments than businesses. Villages are even smaller than towns. Towns and villages have their own shopping and businesses,

Towns and villages have more houses and apartments than businesses.

People are spread out in rural communities. The extra land is shared with animals and crops.

but some people who live in suburbs commute, or travel, to jobs in the city.

Beyond the suburbs are rural communities. A rural community is sometimes called the country or the countryside. It has fewer people living in a much larger area, so its homes and buildings are spread far apart. Much of the land in rural areas is used for agriculture, or farming.

VOCABULARY

Facilities are buildings or other spaces meant for a specific purpose.

Neighborhoods

When people first started moving from country farms into cities, they often decided to live close to others who had similar backgrounds. This was the start of neighborhoods.

Neighborhoods are smaller communities located within cities, towns, and villages. Town neighborhoods are located on a street or two. Neighborhoods in big cities may be spread across several blocks or even a few miles. Sometimes neighborhoods are known for a geographical

Neighborhoods in small towns may consist of the homes on only a few streets.

COMPARE AND CONTRAST
Other than size, in what ways might city neighborhoods be different than town neighborhoods?

feature such as a lake or a hill. Many large cities, such as New York and Los Angeles, have ethnic neighborhoods. These neighborhoods have many people from one particular culture living and working in them.

Neighborhoods can also be defined by the social activities of the people that live there or by how much money the people have.

San Francisco's Chinatown is a well-known ethnic neighborhood in California.

COMMUNITY CENTERS

Community centers are places where people gather to spend time together and participate in activities. The main purpose of a community center is to develop and improve a neighborhood.

The first community center was founded in 1884. It was called Toynbee Hall and was located in a poor area of London, England. University students worked with community members to improve the living conditions of their neighborhood.

The first community center in the United States opened in New York City in

◀◀ London's Toynbee Hall was the first known community center in the world.

THINK ABOUT IT

Some communities have resource centers, such as food pantries. What is the difference between community centers and resource centers?

1886. Others soon followed in cities such as Chicago and Boston.

Today's community centers provide services meant to improve living conditions for members of the surrounding community. They offer classes and activities for adults and children. These activities include things like music and sports.

Community centers may also offer other services for the people of a neighborhood. These services can include health care and job training.

A nurse checks the health of a visitor to a community center for the aged.

COMMUNITY OF IDENTITY

Identity is a collection of features that make someone who they are. These features include age and gender. How and where someone is raised, the kind of schooling he or she receives, and other life experiences also can affect identity. Some communities are made up of people who share some of those features.

A community of identity brings together people who share one or more qualities or experiences. For instance, people are part of a community based on their gender or gender identity. They may

These girls belong to a community based on the fact they have the same gender.

Gospel singers share more than a love of music. They also have a shared religious culture.

share experiences and feel part of a community with other people who identify as their same gender.

Culture also affects identity. Culture is a pattern of behavior shared by a group of people. It involves shared food, language, clothing, music, customs, beliefs, and religion. Communities of identity may be made up of people from the same culture.

FAMILY AS A COMMUNITY

A family is the most basic kind of community. It is the first kind that most people experience. A family is two or more people connected by biology, adoption, marriage, or strong emotions. A family can be considered a type of community of identity because people's identities are shaped, in part, by their families.

Members of a family are part of a community based on their relationships with each other. Families

Two parents and their child make up just one kind of family unit, or community.

Spending time together can make a family a strong community.

regularly share resources, such as food, water, and electricity. Family members often combine their money in order to be able to afford these types of resources.

Family members also regularly interact with one another—hopefully in mainly good ways. The family is one of the best ways people give and receive love and support.

THINK ABOUT IT

Extended family members are people who are related to each other but normally do not live together. What relatives are considered extended members of your family community?

SHARED INTERESTS

Another way communities form is when people share a common interest. In this type of community, members do not need to live close to each other.

People share many different kinds of interests. Some young people enjoy scouting. Adults who were part of a scouting troop when they were younger may choose to continue to be a part of that community by being a scout leader. Playing in the school band shows community spirit through music. People who collect and swap trading

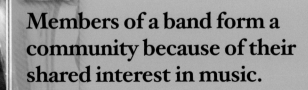

Members of a band form a community because of their shared interest in music.

People who enjoy playing together form a kind of community.

COMPARE AND CONTRAST
Some communities of interest might gather to support a cause or help others. How are activities in these communities different or the same as those in other communities of interest?

cards belong to a community that is interested in a particular type of card game. Likewise, those who love soccer, and play every chance they get, can be considered part of a soccer community.

School Communities

Schools have the qualities of many kinds of communities. They can be considered geographic communities because students often go to schools in or near their neighborhood.

Schools run by religious organizations could be thought of as communities of identity. The teachers and the students share certain beliefs that define who they

School communities are made up of all the kids in every grade.

are. All-boy and all-girl schools can also be communities of identity.

Finally, schools can be called communities of interest. For example, students with an interest in, or talent for, music or theater might choose

School plays are a chance for those who like theater to share an artistic experience.

to attend a school for the arts. Mostly, though, it is because both teachers and students share an interest in learning.

THINK ABOUT IT

Schools all over the world share the same purpose— to educate students. In a sense, then, all schools are part of a worldwide learning community.

THE GLOBAL COMMUNITY

As you learned earlier, geographic communities are groups of people who live in a certain area. Each geographic community can be part of a bigger community. For example, a neighborhood is part of a city. Cities, suburbs, and urban areas are also part of larger areas called states or provinces. Those states and provinces are parts of countries.

Students explore a map showing different countries, or world communities.

People of all races, genders, and cultures make up the global community.

Countries around the world are part of the global community. They work together through organizations such the United Nations. They also sell goods to one another.

Because we all share the planet, individual people all over the world are also members of the global community. Working together, we can make the global community a great place to be.

COMPARE AND CONTRAST
Countries are not called local communities. What makes these places different from local communities such as neighborhoods and cities?

GLOSSARY

band To gather together.

boundary A dividing line; something that shows a limit or end.

climate The average weather conditions of a place or region.

culture A pattern of behavior shared by a group of people.

ethnic Of or relating to groups of people with common traits and customs and a sense of shared identity.

geographic Having to do with the natural features of a place.

global Involving the entire world.

goods Objects or products that people can buy and use.

identity The qualities that make a particular person or group different from others.

interact Talking or doing something with other people.

quality A basic feature that someone or something has.

resource Something that can be used by people.

services Things that people do for others.

transportation The way in which people travel from one place to another.

urban Of or relating to cities.

FOR MORE INFORMATION

Books

Ajmera, Maya and John D. Ivanko. *Be My Neighbor.* Watertown, MA: Charlesbridge, 2004.

Cane, Ella. *Communities in My World.* North Mankato, MN: Capstone Press, 2014.

Caseley, Judith. *On the Town: A Community Adventure.* New York, NY: Greenwillow Books, 2002.

Kalman, Bobbie. *What Is a Community from A to Z?* New York, NY: Crabtree Publishing, 2000.

Sterling, Kristin. *Living in Urban Communities.* Minneapolis, MN: Lerner Books, 2008.

Websites

Because of the changing nature of internet links, Rosen Publishing has developed an online list of websites related to the subject of this book. This site is updated regularly. Please use this link to access the list:

http://www.rosenlinks.com/LFO/communities

INDEX